GW00585657

The
BHUTANESE
GUIDE
to HAPPINESS

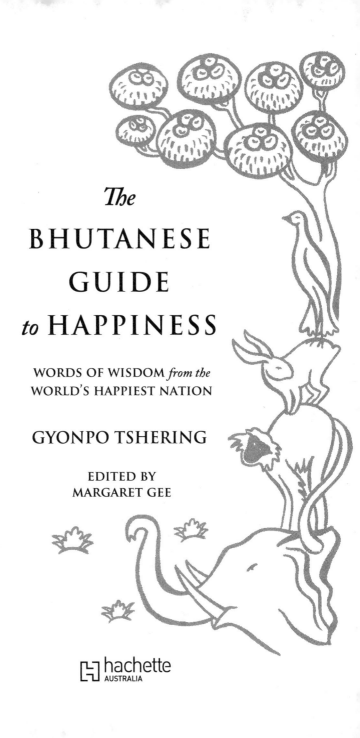

The

BHUTANESE
GUIDE
to HAPPINESS

WORDS OF WISDOM *from the*
WORLD'S HAPPIEST NATION

GYONPO TSHERING

EDITED BY
MARGARET GEE

hachette
AUSTRALIA

hachette
AUSTRALIA

Published in Australia and New Zealand in 2013
by Hachette Australia
(an imprint of Hachette Australia Pty Limited)
Level 17, 207 Kent Street, Sydney NSW 2000
www.hachette.com.au

10 9 8 7 6 5 4 3 2 1

Offset by arrangement with Penguin Ananda, Penguin Books India, 2013

Copyright © Gyonpo Tshering 2013
Foreword copyright © Her Majesty Ashi Dorji Wangmo Wangchuck,
  Queen Mother of Bhutan 2013
Introduction copyright © Margaret Gee 2013

This book is copyright. Apart from any fair dealing for the purposes of private study,
research, criticism or review permitted under the *Copyright Act 1968*, no part
may be stored or reproduced by any process without prior written permission.
Enquiries should be made to the publisher.

National Library of Australia
Cataloguing-in-Publication data:

Tshering, Gyonpo.
The Bhutanese guide to happiness / Gyonpo Tshering, edited by Margaret Gee.

978 0 7336 3199 3 (pbk.)

Happiness – Quotations, maxims, etc.
Happiness – Popular works.
Inspiration – Quotations, maxims, etc.
Bhutan – Quotations, maxims, etc.

Tshering, Gyonpo, compiler.
Gee, Margaret, editor.

158.1

Cover illustration by Joy Gosney
Cover design by Gavin Morris
Internal illustrations by Chetan Kishore
Digital production by Bookhouse, Sydney
Printed and bound in Australia by Griffin Press, Adelaide, an Accredited ISO AS/NZS
14001:2009 Environmental Management System printer

MIX
Paper from
responsible sources
FSC
www.fsc.org   **FSC® C009448**

The paper this book is printed on is certified against the
Forest Stewardship Council® Standards. Griffin Press holds
FSC chain of custody certification SGS-COC-005088. FSC
promotes environmentally responsible, socially beneficial
and economically viable management of the world's forests.

The Bhutanese Guide to Happiness is dedicated to
the fifth coronation anniversary of
His Majesty the King Jigme Khesar Namgyel Wangchuck,
for bringing unprecedented economic prosperity, social
harmony, and happiness under his glorious reign.

FOREWORD

Gyonpo Tshering's collection of proverbs is from the land of Gross National Happiness (GNH)—a concept that originated from the wise mind and compassionate heart of His Majesty Jigme Singye Wangchuck, the fourth king of Bhutan.

His unique philosophy guides as well as measures Bhutan's growth and progress not by its Gross Domestic Product but by its GNH. It is based on the conviction that material wealth alone does not bring happiness or ensure the wellbeing of its people, and that economic growth and 'modernisation' should not be at the expense of the people's quality of life. Bhutan's philosophy of governance based on GNH, which is now acclaimed by economists and planners the world over, also reflects the spiritual and cultural values that have guided Bhutan through the ages. Many of these values are echoed in this collection of Bhutanese proverbs.

Full of timeless wisdom and universal truths, these proverbs were passed down orally to us by our ancestors.

My own grandfather was a fount of folk wisdom, and used to recite his favourite proverbs to us in our childhood. I am happy that Gyonpo Tshering has compiled some of the best of our proverbs into this book so that they can reach a wide readership.

'Life is like footprints in the snow. Every step will show', says one of the proverbs in Gyonpo Tshering's collection—a short and simple saying which, like other proverbs in this book, conveys a profound message. I hope this volume will be a valued companion in the reader's journey to a happier life, and be enjoyed and appreciated for years to come.

Ashi Dorji Wangmo Wangchuck
Queen Mother of Bhutan

INTRODUCTION

Bhutan is flanked by India, China and Tibet—a tiny jewel of a country nestled in the Eastern Himalayas between two immense superpowers. This position may make it seem vulnerable, but its values—a devotion to the highest principles of human existence—give it strength.

Bhutan is the first and only country in the world to have a government edict that Gross National Happiness (GNH) is more important than Gross Domestic Product. The principal of GNH—emphasising a selfless service to others and the search for enlightenment—is a core value of this unique Buddhist kingdom. They have a designated Gross National Happiness centre—a magnet for scholars and experts studying this innovative philosophy—which will spread this message to a wider, troubled world.

The concept of GNH has received international media coverage and 'happiness' conferences seem to be springing up worldwide. The current Prime Minister of Bhutan, Jigmi Y. Thinley, addressed the United Nations in New York on the concept of GNH. Bhutan has a lot it can teach us.

Bhutan is entirely original. It appears at first glance to be a simple country with a village-based subsistence lifestyle. Yet beneath the surface, it is a rich, diverse community comprising groups such as yak herders and the nomadic Laya people as well as a complex royal and government hierarchy, overseen by scholars, gurus, rinpoches, high Lamas, abbots, senior monks, and some of the most environmentally devout practitioners in the world. (Bhutan is the only country in the world to have banned cigarette smoking and was the first to ban plastic bags in 1999.)

The landscape is dotted with houses decorated with flowers and Buddhist art *dzongs* (fortresses) and *chortens* (a type of pagoda), and innumerable monasteries. The most famous of these is the stunning Tiger's Nest or Taktshang Monastery, which clings to the steep hillsides in the upper Paro Valley, surrounded by blue pine and spruce forests. The revered Guru Padmasambhava, who is credited with introducing Buddhism to Bhutan, is said to have meditated here for three months in the eighth century AD.

Even if you have a secular or agnostic view of religion, it is hard not to be moved by the intense and highly visible Buddhist practices, ceremonies, monuments, stories, festivals, fables, chants, incantations and offerings to their gods, goddesses, and other deities that are an everyday part of Bhutanese life.

The Bhutanese people appear to live the way of loving kindness and compassion—the major tenets of the Mahayana Buddhism to which they subscribe. They also have a great capacity for jokes and laughter. They seem to live in the moment, and have as their highest priorities, community, family and faith.

From the time I arrive until I leave, I feel happier in Bhutan than anywhere else on the planet, and cannot seem to wipe the smile off my face!

Perhaps it will be the wisdom from one of the smallest and happiest nations on earth, Bhutan, that will ultimately provide the necessary guidance for stability and peace so longed for throughout the world.

Like every great journey, the first step begins with us. Gyonpo Tshering and I sincerely hope that *The Bhutanese Guide to Happiness* will illuminate your own path to enhanced happiness, tranquillity and wellbeing.

Tashi Delek
Margaret Gee

The

BHUTANESE
GUIDE
to HAPPINESS

Human life is like a butter lamp
flickering in the wind.

Proverbs are a garland of
ancient precious jewels to wear
around the mind and heart.

Like there is no beam
without a supporting pillar,
there can be no education
without a strong teacher.

The seedlings of spiritual
devotion are hit hard by the
hailstorm of laziness.

If you search for happiness, you will not find it. If happiness searches for you, it will always find you.

The sunshine of a Lama's mandala is necessary to remove the darkness of spiritual unawareness.

A flea springs up from
a cozy blanket,
A hero springs up from
a rocky ledge.

A yak herder takes the credit,
but it is the poor yak which
carries the heavy load.

Cold weather doesn't care if
your coat is old or new.

The milk of the snow leopard
is nectar from the gods of the
Himalayas.

A king can only do so much to
protect a lawbreaker, as a Lama
can do to protect a sinner.

The doctor's son can get ill
and even the astrologer's horse
can get lost.

When you have climbed hard
to the mountain pass, you will
be rewarded with the sight of a
flowery meadow.

If the company you keep
encourages you to steal, your
moral compass has already
been stolen.

Without a blessed life, even gold
or silver have no value.

A person who cannot keep their
promises is like a tree with a
rotting trunk.

Even a howling snowstorm
will not silence the melody of a
lark's voice.

Singing a song with a clear and
open mind is better than
reciting a mantra with a bad
attitude.

Even if a cup breaks, don't
forget the beautiful pattern on it.

If you don't understand the
true meaning of the
Buddha's sutras and tantras,
you will just be reciting the texts
like a parrot.

Pile up good deeds in this life,
and in the next life you will have
mountains of happiness.

If you say nasty things about
people, sooner or later you will
meet your victim face-to-face.

When a fool makes a mistake,
the pond ripples.
When a learned scholar makes a mistake,
there can be a tidal wave.

A white lion can be famous,
but only a loyal guard dog can
protect your house.

If you have not experienced
great suffering and great
happiness, you will find
it hard to tell them apart.

Suffering always ends, and so
does happiness.

Do not chirrup too much about
your happiness, and do not
whine too much about your
unhappiness.

Parents are like walnuts,
hard on the outside and soft
on the inside.

Happiness and suffering are like
the summer sun. One moment
it is shining, and the next
it is covered by dark clouds.

There is one moment of
human birth, but a hundred
ways to die.

Growing old physically is not true old age—that only comes with growing old mentally.

People who are not careful about what they say tend not to be careful with the rest of their body.

The wind never stops blowing
and the river never rests.

Profits in your hand can mean
a loss will soon be dropped at
your feet.

A rich heart is better than
money in the bank.

It is better to die among the
prudent and conscientious
than among the reckless and
shameless.

An elephant wishes he could jump like a flea, and a flea wishes he could be strong like an elephant.

It is better to be a wise owl than a cunning monkey.

A rope can bind just one, but a harsh law can bind millions.

Anger is a golden opportunity to practise patience.

If a female dog does not wag its tail, a male dog will not perk up his ears.

The sun is the greatest jewel of all.

The frog in the pond is doomed
if he only dreams of swimming
in the ocean.

A man or woman without a
good legacy is like a horse which
has become lame.

If you fly on the wings of a
drunken eagle, you will very
soon fall to the ground.

In the bed of a high achiever
you will find the corpse of an
ordinary person.

If you quarrel, the gods will
trouble you. If you are friendly,
the demons will leave you alone.

If you find someone who loves
you as much as your parents,
you are sure to have
a happy family.

We are all shepherds, so learn
how to tend kindly
to your flock.

Angrily rebuking a quiet and
thoughtful person is like
trampling on the petals of a rose.

Leaves rustling in a gentle breeze is the same sound as the voice of a goddess.

Tigers have stripes on the outside, people have stripes within.

If you are happy in your home,
even when you are away,
you will never feel homesick.

When people tell lies, their souls
begin to crumble.

It is better to plant flowers than
to build monuments.

When a bad thing happens, you
feel like a rock plummeting
down a crevasse.

Even if the tap runs dry,
you can always count on it
raining again soon.

If two old friends reconcile
it should be like two rivers
meeting, a waterfall of affection
and happiness.

Speaking out of turn is like
wearing ill-fitting clothes.

A good king can take you to the
top of the mountain, but a bad
one will push you over the edge.

Make sure you can tell the
difference between the prints of
a tiger and a domestic cat.

If your leader turns into a dog,
be sure to ask why he is
wagging his tail.

You cannot broaden your
horizons by staying at home,
or spare the oceans
without saving water.

Even though an ant appears to
be small and weak, it has
the strength and determination
of a buffalo.

Just as the peacock can change
its colours,
a monk can transform offerings.

During bad times,
good friends are essential.
During good times,
bad friends are still unnecessary.

Do not expect a donkey to be able to carry the same load as an elephant.

You can create your own happiness or your own misery.

Even the sun can be eclipsed,
so be aware of
your own limitations.

A man who wears a dog mask
will not roar like a lion.
A man wearing a lion mask will
not bark like a dog.

The wisdom of our ancestors
will be there for as long as a
crow's feathers are black.

People who go on acquiring
things they don't need might
eventually lose everyone
they value.

Negative thoughts can
so easily slip into
negative and destructive actions.

Even while it sleeps, the cat
dreams of the mouse.

A fool rushes across a field of
snow, but a wise person first
makes sure there are
no holes to fall into.

You don't need sunshine to
warm your good fortune.
It should, by itself, warm
your heart and soul.

If you don't communicate well,
you will disturb the minds of
others. If you don't know how
to listen you will disturb
your own mind.

If you take an oath lightly,
one day it could
weigh you down.

Don't become obsessed with making a mountain of money, otherwise you will fall into an abyss of despair.

What we have already achieved is the size of a fingernail, what is left for others to do is your height from head to toe.

The temple may be ancient,
but the meaning is always modern.

A demon you know is better
than an unknown deity.

A human being abandoned by a
Lama feels like a tree that
has been uprooted.

Saying nasty things about other
people is as odious
as smelly shoes.

Don't cross a swiftly flowing
river unless you want to end up
drifting helplessly in the ocean.

You should protect your
possessions, but if something is
stolen, perhaps someone needed
the object more than you.

Real intelligence is not about
what you say, but how you
behave towards others.

One dream cannot rest
on two pillows.

Evil words are like
poisonous flowers.
Evil actions are like
poisonous roots.

It is more important to have
good teeth in your head
than a hat which
fits properly on it.

You cannot be gentle like a beautiful tree if your tongue cuts others like an axe.

Kind words sow the seeds of the lotus. Cruel words sow the seeds of poison ivy.

If you take a wrong path you can
turn around, but harsh words
can never be taken back.

A dragon's roar is soon forgotten,
but a rainbow's beauty
lasts forever.

It is better to cherish a swiftly
flowing river than to run off at
the mouth like a drain.

When arguments are settled
with money everyone is
impoverished.

If disputes are not peacefully
resolved, the volcano will
continue to erupt.

If you don't repay your debts
you will be repaid
with bad karma.

A bribe is like a moustache, it
covers the truth
beneath the skin.

Truth is medicine.
Lying is poison.

Empty words are like empty
plates. They make people
hungry for
genuine nourishment.

Sweets are as delicious to eat as
proverbs are delectable to hear.

Your health will be better if you
receive a blessing from a Lama.

If your aspirations
are unrealistically high,
you may emotionally spiral
out of control.

The wisdom of India, Bhutan
and Tibet can cleanse your
soul, but you have to make the
decision to journey to these
spiritual countries.

In the same way that there is
gold in the earth,
there is Buddha nature in
all sentient beings.

A happy life is like the blink of an eye, but a miserable life is a never-ending journey.

When faced with imminent danger, a regal tiger will tremble just as much as a street dog.

People who are mean with money are usually mean with their love and friendship.

Life is like footprints in the snow. Every step will show.

If you are always on a fishing
expedition for a better life, the
surface of your spiritual ocean
will never be calm.

Your God will always support
you, but ultimately you are on
your own spiritual journey.

No gold in the ground can ever
be more beautiful
than a sunbeam.

You can choose not to speak, but
it is impossible to silence idle
chatter in the streets.

No trader could ever make
money selling bad behaviour.

If you are honest, the birds in
the sky will befriend you. If you
are dishonest, your own son or
daughter will avoid you.

Just when you get the hang of
being young, old age taps you
on the shoulder.

Happiness comes from
mental freedom.
Suffering comes from
an emotional prison.

If you value your own life, don't take the life of other sentient creatures.

If you don't think for yourself, your mouth will broadcast the will of others.

Be calm and dignified if you are
ever invited to the palace of a
powerful king; therein lies the
way of mutual respect.

When luck favours us,
the blessings of the Lamas
have borne fruit.

Your children are the fire and
light in your heart.

Your father's work often looks
easy, as your mother's delicious
cooking can seem easy too.
Both happen because of
skill and hard work.

Knowledge is a useful pathway,
but experience will get you to
the destination faster.

As your age travels to the
highest mountain peaks,
your backbone bends
towards the valley.

If you don't deliver a parcel,
you are a thief.
If you don't deliver a message,
then also you are a thief.

Talk without experience and
practice is like a bird
with no feathers.

You have to walk the talk
otherwise your religious devotion
is a stagnant river.

A single terrible lie may cost you
someone's lifelong trust.

It is more important to think
well of your lifetime partner
than to feel affection for a
passing stranger.

If you roll in the muck of life,
you will never purify your soul.

Your karmic destiny book
is already written.

As there is a different language
for each valley in Bhutan, there
is a different religious practice
for each Lama.

When the valleys of the mind
are flooded, even the sacred
retreat caves will not save you.

Live simply.
Leave only footprints and
carry only your shadow.
This is the way.

I would rather have a university degree than an ornate piece of jewellery which could be stolen.

When the karmic wind blows, the karmic rain is not far away.

The body does not want to
be polluted with disease as
the mind does not want to be
muddy with sorrow.

If you have a calm mind, your
body will be tranquil.
If your body is calm then it will
help to calm your mind.

Quality, not quantity, is the key
to happiness.

A bad harvest can be replanted
and yield a good crop.
A bad partner is
harder to replace.

A poor harvest lasts a year,
but cruel words can resonate
for a lifetime.

Even if we are told we only have
a few years to live, we still need
to employ the wisdom passed
down through the ages.

Life is short, but education lasts
at least a hundred years.

It is folly to forget that you are
merely human, and to lust after
the wealth of celestial beings.

Telling secrets is like spilling
melted butter.

If you hurt someone you love,
it is like a fingernail being
torn from flesh.

Just the way vegetables taste
better with cheese,
human beings are happier
living as couples
than surviving alone.

The eyes of the beloved deceased
will still watch you
in the afterlife.

Don't tell everybody everything.
Have respect for your privacy
and innermost thoughts.

Don't make your will as soon as
you get sick—it could hasten
your passing away.

We all emerge from the Eastern
pass at birth and depart from the
Western pass in death.

Be like the sun and always rise,
and the country stream which
keeps gently flowing.

If you have no debts,
you are rich,
and if you have no quarrels,
you are happier.

When the dawn breaks,
the world smiles
with happiness and joy.

The tree and the mushroom
will rot together, and the
meadow and the flower
will fade together.

What is more beautiful than the
sun illuminating a mountain
with a pink-and-orange glow,
or a bird singing happily
in a treetop?

If you have something on your
mind, get it out—
just as it is important
to remove grubs
eating the bark of a tree.

One lie will vanquish
a hundred truths.

A muddy sty is a palace to a pig.

Not everything you hear is true,
nor all unpleasant things the
enemy of your happiness.

Explanations don't always solve
the mysteries of life,
as crying does not always heal
the pain of sadness.

Some things are only written on
the paper of the mind.

If there is no inner contentment,
it doesn't help even if your path
is strewn with diamonds.

If you throw a stone at a bird,
your sky may fall in.

Just as there are green, fertile
pastures and barren plains,
the same is true for the territory
of the heart and mind.

You can never completely trust
the human mind until
true enlightenment is attained.

Be like a wild animal and have
an acute sense of smell for
danger.

Even if some people saw a
Buddha flying in the sky,
they would not have faith
in what they have seen.
In the same way, some people will
not have compassion even if
they see a poor animal
suffering in a field.

Every king has one evil minister,
just as each Buddha
has a demon.

Practise the dharma for the
sake of enlightenment,
as you raise your children to
love and respect you.

It is a bad thing in the court of
life if the verdict is passed before
the witness has spoken.

Telling proverbs to old people
is as insulting as teaching
the alphabet to the Buddha.

Even though the Buddha has
the hook of genuine guidance,
people without faith will not
hang their hats on it.

If you find a piece of turquoise
at your doorstep, it is a very
auspicious omen. If you find an
animal on the high mountain,
he may carry you safely down.

A snow leopard reigns supreme
in the mountains but is
sometimes treated like a
stray dog in the village.

We are what we are.
A tiger does not try to be
a lion and vice versa.

It is more important to
have a beautiful mind,
than a beautiful face.

You don't have to smile if you
are pleased, nor do you have
to frown if you are displeased.
People who do this don't get so
many wrinkles!

Thoughts roam around like a
galloping horse, instead of being
contained in the palm
of your hand.

A fickle mind, two-faced
behaviour and a lying nature:
these three can never be friends.

Limiting your eating is good for your health, and not fighting with your wife or husband is good for your heart.

Too much food can be poisonous to your health, and too much anger can poison your friendships.

Good spiritual connections
lead to Buddhahood,
and bad spiritual connections
lead to Hell.

If you are given a jug of
good wine, repay the favour
with fresh water
from a mountain spring.
Both are enriching.

Money doesn't make people
happy, but neither does poverty.
Share what you have
for a better world.

People who roar like tigers
at home, and are sweet as
pussycats in public, will
always scratch you.

Eating and loving are natural,
but the right teacher can give you
some good tips for making it
a better experience.

If there are too many carpenters,
the door may not shut properly.

Evil is the vilest type of hatred,
and patience the most
sought-after virtue.

It is all right to let go of the moon,
for the mandala of the sun will still
rise in the morning.

People with good manners
argue about seating, people with
bad manners argue about what
food is being served.

How you behave
is the barometer of
your good manners.

The voices of your ancestors
will echo in the valley
of your heart, forever.

We never see where the arrow
came from, only where it lands.

Pray that the wisdom eyes of
the Buddha look upon you,
otherwise you are at the whim
of the world.

The eyes of true wisdom never
stray across the horizon.

Even if you were only in
the company of the Buddha,
you would probably
quarrel sometimes.

Don't throw mud into someone
else's unpolluted stream.

Learn how to be happy with a few garments instead of lusting for a wardrobe full of luxurious clothes. Like the tiger, we can only wear one coat at a time.

Sometimes the poorest people are the most generous, and the richest in spirit.

It is better to sit at the feet of the
learned, than to be at the head
of a table of idiots.

Only arrogant people think that
arrogance is an admirable trait.

Be like a tree: sway and bend,
but never break.

If someone says they have no
faults then there is
probably something seriously wrong
with them.

Nomads are the most skilled at
finding the best pastures, and
villagers are the most skilled at
pleasing the deities.

Every man or woman has their
own way of thinking,
and every village has its own
traditions and customs.

If you become wealthy through dishonesty, don't expect it to last. Your bad deeds will catch up with you.

If you are unhappy, even a beautiful summer's day will feel like the cold heart of winter.

A herd of goats will have trouble toppling a strong tree, and bad people will find it hard to bring down a good person.

If farm animals have proper shelter, a hawk will not be happy in its mountain nest.

When a goat is killed,
the sheep shivers.

A happy man in filthy rags
is richer than a miserable
merchant dressed in finery.

Like high mountains seeing
others but never meeting, some
kindred spirits are destined
to live apart.

The higher the mountain,
the deeper the abyss.
The greater the gain,
the more potential for loss.
The deeper the dharma,
the more numerous are the obstacles.

A great mountain will not be
moved by wind, and a great
ocean cannot be burned by fire.

Like a wild animal always
wanting more meat, human
desire is never satisfied.

If people respect each other the way they respect the Buddha, they will have a peaceful life.

Rich and powerful people will desert you if you lose your money and power—there is a lesson to be learned here.

We point a spear at others
even though we cannot bear
our fingers to be pricked
by a needle.

We disguise our mountains of
faults, but find valleys of faults
with others.

If you dispense with negativity,
you are on the Buddhist path.

If it does not ferment,
it is not beer.
If it does not grow and develop,
it is not a true mind.

Intelligence is like fresh snow
on the mountain, and stupidity
is like a forest gutted by fire.

Beware of speeches that have
the same three elements:
'I did not see,' 'I did not know,'
'I was not aware.'

As a stone is wedged in place to
stabilise a pillar, a good mediator
will sort out a dispute.

If you live a long life, you will
experience three kinds of
happiness and three kinds of
suffering.

Don't let your disagreements
outlive you.

Even a small horse can come
from good breeding, and even
if I am short I may still have
descended from Padma Lingpa*.

*The spiritual treasure revealer

A human's happiness is
in its mind, a dog's happiness
is in its tail.

You get to know your horse by
riding it for a long time, as you
get to know people by spending
a lot of time talking with them
and drinking tea.

If actions are not carried out
with a pure heart, it is as if
gold becomes sand.

Even mature people need
guidance, as clever people
need inspiration.

If you become poor and your
relatives reject you, you can only
be enriched by leaving them.

You will only truly realise the
peace and happiness in your
own country when you travel
around the world.

A man may be buried in the
ground, but his words will still
be carried by the winds.

A human without faults
is a Buddha.
A Buddha with faults
is a human.

Unpleasant medicine will
sometimes cure you in the same
way that people you don't
like will sometimes benefit you.

Good people's minds are like
gold, they never change colour.

A good, old dog will protect you
from fierce robbers in the same
way that old people will guard
the wisdom of history.

Don't stare too much with your
eyes, or blare too much
with your mouth.

Even though you climb the
tree of fame and success, you
are not immune from falling to
the ground and breaking your
bones.

As flowers are the ornaments
of the fields, the proverbs
of the scholars are the ornaments
of the community.

If you drink too much of
anything, even mother's milk,
you will get indigestion. If you
hear too much of anything,
you will stop listening
and fall asleep.

Achieving results without
hardship is like saying you
will only eat fish that do not
have scales.

For some, a happy life is
dependent on wealth, but the
happiness of the next life only
depends on the dharma.

Even the most cherished body
in life will become the food of
vultures and worms in the end.

The next life is always longer
than this one, just as the lord of
death is fiercer than
any present ruler.

A tailor is never satisfied with
his alterations, but he is always
satisfied with the leftover
pieces of cloth.

A donkey is burdened by his
heavy load as a shopkeeper is
burdened by always wanting
more customers.

Traders are not always honest
and thieves rarely spend
money wisely.

Wounds made by weapons can heal, wounds made by harsh words leave terrible emotional scars.

Your beloved child can lie to you, and your hated enemy can teach you some wisdom.

Your five fingers are like
brothers and each has its own
hand of fate.

This fickle human life usually
ends with one long sigh and one
long night.

A bad night's sleep can make
you feel tired for ten days.

Your face can have the glow of
a lotus, but your mind can be as
dark as an ink stain.

When you see the person you
love, the sight is rapturous,
and when you hear their voice,
it is like listening to music, and
the devotion grows.

Even if the terms of
a peace treaty cannot be agreed
upon, violent war should
always be avoided.

Words that will hurt another
should be stopped,
like a boulder which is about to
crash on to a building.

If you gloat at others'
misfortunes, you may soon be
mired in your own unhappiness.

A person with high standards
who helps others is like a
king or queen in their own
community.

We can see any physical faults
by looking in the mirror.
But deficits in our inner lives
can only be realised and set on
the right path with genuine
spiritual guidance.

Leftover food becomes
food for rats.
Leftover clothes become
food for moths.

When someone says, 'Come,
eat and drink,' the ears perk up.
When someone says, 'Come to
work,' the ears go flat.

You may enjoy food at other people's houses, but the best bed is always in your own home.

If your wealth disappears, you involuntarily become a yogi.

Some conversations are hard
to start as some tasks are
difficult to conclude.

Giving to others is the gateway
to compassion, but many would
prefer to accumulate possessions
just for themselves.

If you take the jungle away from
a free, roaming snow leopard, it
will feel like a poor street dog.

The more dark clouds
gather on the mountaintop,
the more the water will rage
in the river below.

Tigers have eighteen ways
of leaping, but jackals have
nineteen ways of hiding.

The misfortune of someone
born in the Tiger year is
transferred to someone born
in the Rabbit year.

The more affluent and powerful
you become, the less you should
spoil your children.

Human life is as transient and
impermanent as the setting sun
is on the horizon.

Look carefully, there is a
big difference between
mist and smoke.

If you are committed to a
spiritual life, this and the next
life will be happy. If not,
both will be ruined.

If you are in a beautiful flower-filled meadow you will sing with joy; if you are at the edge of a cliff you will cry out in fear.

Never leave the Lama who shows you the path to liberation until you have attained Buddhahood.

If striving for success fills you with fear, it is better to stay home and meditate.

If you throw dust up into the air, some will fall on others, but most will fall on yourself.

An ocean is a collection of
drops, a rock is a collection of
particles, but they are of equal
value. The same is true for the
love you have in your
heart and mind.

Do not attempt to climb
the mountain unless you
are prepared to fall
down the crevasse.

Virtuous deeds and dire
suffering can both lead to
divine happiness.

Defeat is part of the price you
can pay for victory.

If you don't have horns you are
not a bull, and if you are
not warm and friendly
you can't be happy.

The King of Medicine is Anu,
who says there are more
who die than recover.
The King of Poison is Tsendug,
who says there are more
who recover than die.

Eat in accordance with the seasons as you would dress for different types of weather.

Mushrooms always rise to the surface.

People worry about rich people
who are sick, but forget about
poor people who are dying.

The wealth of the devout goes
to charity. The wealth of the
arrogant goes to the enemy.
The wealth of the miser is
eaten by bugs.

Betel nut, the leaf and the lime—
if one important ingredient is
missing, the flavour is lost,
just like life.

In order to achieve great results,
you have to let go of
minor matters.

Just as the wind knows what is light or heavy, people instinctively know who is of higher or lower ranking.

The fir tree and the bamboo are different plant species, but both grow tall and strong.

An ugly face worries the owner,
and an ugly thought worries
your companion.

The place to distinguish gold
from brass is at the smithy.
The place to distinguish
fact from fiction is
at the courthouse.

Do not seek refuge in demons
and charlatans. Keep your faith
in the protective deities.

The demons are powerful,
but the Buddha's truth
will always prevail.

When there are no fellow archers around, you will be the one shooting the best arrows.

Explain things to people who ask, and teach to those who yearn to learn.

Don't trust a snarling wild dog,
nor trust someone you
don't know.

Hell is close to the grave of a
sinner, and liberation is near the
place of an enlightened one's
departure to the next life.

Rather live a short, happy life
than a long, unhappy one.

When we are ill, it is medicine
which heals us. And when
we are dying, it is the dharma which
is our salvation.

If there were no tigers in the
forest, there would be no end to
monkey business.

If there is no harmony at home,
you will not be successful in the
outside world.

You can die from overeating or hunger. As ever, the best path is always the middle way.

Without inner awareness, the eyes seeing the world might as well be blind.

As a drowning man grabs at anything to save himself, so a liar will say anything to salvage his reputation.

Just like you would not be picky with food if you were starving, do not be choosy with doctors if you are seriously ill.

Be aware of the power of the
gods, but don't ignore the
presence of the devils.

When you have the wealth of a rat,
you will also have the
suffering of a rat.
When you have the wealth of a horse,
you will also have the
suffering of a horse.

When a jewel is in your hand,
you don't value it. That only
happens when you lose
it to someone else.

Just as anything can grow well
in a summer meadow,
anything can happen in the
yogi's experience.

The greatest wealth is
generosity, and the most
sublime happiness is to reach
the state of bodhicitta*.

If you don't cultivate a good
mind, it will disappear like a
shooting star in the sky.

* 'Bodhicitta' in Buddhism means being able to
bring happiness to all sentient beings

If you want to put great ideas
into action, you need to apply the
strength of a Himalayan mountain.

If you are a true monk,
you will not be greedy,
and if you are a true yogi,
you will be free of fixed ideas.

The cause of both happiness and sorrow is the result of your previous actions.

Telling other people what to do is easy, telling yourself what to do is very difficult.

A hero in battle can overcome
one, a hero in learning can
conquer a generation.

The children of a loving mother
are as happy as the subjects
of a Bodhisattva*.

*Enlightened being

You should not bow to every
ruler, or seek empowerments
from every Lama.

A benevolent ruler is prized by
his subjects in the same way that
a good Lama is praised by
divine beings.

Don't fear the ruler, only fear
his power.

If you ask a favour from a king,
the decision as to whether or
not it will be granted will
most likely come from
his trusted attendant.

You cannot eliminate the
wrinkles on your face,
nor can you erase any of
your past actions.

The stillness of a lion is
better than the scampering
of a monkey.

The beggar endures the
suffering of hunger,
and the rich man endures the
suffering of a hoarder.

Just like pearls come from the
ocean, most reincarnated beings
are born into the families
of Lamas.

A father's son is like a white
snow lion, even if the child ends
up behaving like a village dog.

Having loving parents is no
guarantee that your fate will go
in a similarly positive direction.

If you abandon or are unkind to your parents, you will ruin your life and the next one.

Sons of the same father can have different ways of living, just as those sharing a pillow will have different dreams.

Happiness, as you grow up,
is like the phases of the moon—
it waxes and wanes.

When your parents are alive,
you are not always aware of
their affection. After they die,
you always feel their love.

Don't take responsibility for
someone who cannot take
responsibility for themselves.

An authentic person will speak
when necessary.
A mediocre person will speak
when questioned.
A lesser person will only speak
behind your back.

As it takes a while to break in a new horse, so it takes a while for an inexperienced person to learn how to tell good stories.

Even if a man is not well off he must provide, but if a woman is well off she must still receive.

Even if a piglet could dance,
it would not be considered
a ballerina.

If a relative doesn't help you,
they are a stranger. If a stranger
helps you, they are like a
good relative.

The rich inheritance of good parents can be the source of gambling money for degenerate offspring.

Speak in accordance with your audience, and cook in accordance with the ingredients in your larder.

Wars are fought and won by ordinary soldiers, but it is the chief who receives all the adulation.

During the harvesting of sweet buckwheat, both the master and servant should pitch in equally.

Even hawks and eagles must
sometimes touch the ground.

While you are looking for a
needle outside, you will be more
likely to lose the axe at home.

Army chiefs almost always live
longer than their soldiers.

In public, a man can be the
favourite of his officer; and in
private, he can be the sweetheart
of the officer's wife.

Outside dirt can be removed
by washing, but inner dirt
cannot always be removed
by explanation.

If wealthy people do not practise
generosity, in the end they will
be the caretaker of that property
for others.

Wanting more money makes the rich work more, and wanting more food makes the beggar work.

You cannot eat tsampa* and play the flute at the same time.

*Flour and water

Protect your possessions from a
robber, but give your things
to a beggar.

Better to milk the cow and
drink that milk, than kill the
cow and eat its meat.

Bad children do not remember the time of their parents' death, and bad parents do not remember the time of their childrens' birth.

If you have no son then get a son-in-law, and if you have no daughter then get a daughter-in-law.

Bribes and presents are tempting for some judges in the same way that women are tempting for some holy men.

The donkey has many ways of sleeping, but his owner has many ways of making him work.

When birds get old, they look for their nests. When people get old, they want to be home.

Just as the old tortoise loses the shine on his shell, so the demented person lacks his sharpness of mind.

Until enlightenment is attained,
you rely on your spiritual master.
When enlightenment is attained,
you are equal.

In a house with no cats,
mice reign supreme.

If the Lama is allowed to kill the chicken, it will encourage his attendant to steal the eggs.

A student may listen to the Lama's teaching about the dharma, but may still only have blind faith.

For the powerful, there is power,
but little intelligence.
For the intelligent, there is
intelligence, but little power.

Too many chant masters will
distort the ritual as too many
judges will distort the verdict.

Anything can grow in a fertile
meadow, and anything can arise
in an unstable mind.

The sound of thunder is loud,
but it is empty. The rainbow
has pretty colours, but soon
vanishes into emptiness.

Although the takin* dies thin, it
still weighs many yak loads.
But if the rat dies healthy, it can
still fit into your hand.

Just like snake coils are
released by movement, so
the knots in the mind will be
released by repentance.

*Himalayan buck

A yogi should not linger at the
wealthy devotee's house.

Speaking without an audience is
like an echo in an empty cave.

If an ordinary man holds his head high, it is hard for an official to put him down.

If you don't contemplate those who suffer, compassion is just an empty word.

Give someone a bedroom to
sleep in and they may wish to
dwell in your other rooms.

Just as you should not drink
too much tea before bedtime,
do not talk too much
on your deathbed.

Looking for faults in the
innocent is like looking for
corners on an egg.

Dreams without sleeping are
like galloping without a horse.

Don't reply when you are
feeling sleepy, and don't repent
when you are dying.

With close family, even a small
meal is very nourishing, as
things once decided don't have
to be discussed in more detail.

A poor field will one day yield a bumper crop, as a disappointing relative will one day do the right thing by you.

A group of young male deer travelling together may have different lengths of antlers, but they will leave the same hoofprints.

Some gains are a genuine
step forward, others are the
beginning of a nightmare.

If you speak your mind too
openly, you may end up
covering your lips with your
hands in regret.

Sometimes the only things a
poor man has left is an empty
mouth and and an empty hand.

Whenever you ride your horse,
be aware that there are ants
on the ground.

You cannot put two saddles
on one horse, nor can there be
two great masters for
one doctrine.

Before mounting a saddled
horse, pat the saddle
three times.

Better to be thrown by a horse,
than to be thrown out by a king.

When a mare is frisky, it will
chase the stallion; and when a
woman wants her husband, she
sings a song.

A donkey can block a horse's path, and a devil can block a Buddhist practitioner's path.

If you can't be ahead of a hundred horses, don't get behind a hundred donkeys.

Crows will pick out the eyes of a horse before it dies, just as the wealth of a person can be taken before they die.

We don't have enough eyes for all that can be seen, or enough thoughts for everything that can be contemplated.

The most delicious food is inside the basket, like the best lovemaking is under the quilt!

Food left uneaten can be reheated later, but words left unsaid can leave a sour taste in the mouth.

Big celebrations last for one day,
but a family argument can last
for much longer.

If you are starving, do not sell
the family home; and if you are
thirsty, do not drink alcohol—
just water.

Without humour, poor
conversation will result.
Without careful preparation,
your spiritual practice will have
no meaning.

Churn milk a hundred times
and you will make butter;
speak a mantra a hundred times
and you will distill the essence.

Timeless words of wisdom are like messages inscribed on a rock—even if the rock breaks, the wisdom remains.

Totally honest house guests are rare, just as judges rarely give completely honest verdicts.

Pots without handles are hard to hold, in the same way that complicated metaphors are hard to understand.

Gossip passed on usually gathers momentum, but food passed on always decreases.

Words are not weapons, but they can still shatter the heart.

Our last words are our will, and our last clothes are our burial cloths.

Digging into the meaning of
words is like digging in mud.
The deeper you go, the more
you will find.

Name' Same', Kadin Chhe' Chhe'
Thank you, beyond the sky and
the earth.

Gyonpo Tshering is currently Research Specialist at the National Library of Bhutan in the capital city of Thimpu, where he lives. He has a BA in Buddhist philosophy from Semtokha Rigzhung Institute and has translated and written a number of books on Bhutanese history and religion.

Margaret Gee is a keen adventure traveller with a special interest in Asiatic cultures and Buddhist philosophy. Margaret is the coeditor of *Everest: Reflections From The Top.*